Contents

Weight Watchers & the ProPoints PLAN

Food is our fuel, and it's all around us every day. It's time to put yourself back in control of the food choices you make. Weight Watchers gives you a simple, flexible plan to help you achieve this. You can adapt the plan according to your personal preference – whether you want to take a simple approach or a more flexible approach, the choice is yours.

Get the most out of this cookbook

Whether you're on a Filling & Healthy day approach, or you are counting the *ProPoints* values of everything you eat and drink, this cookbook will give you inspiring ways to cook delicious food no matter where you are on your journey.

♥ Filling & Healthy day

If you see a little green heart beside any of the recipes in this book this means it is suitable if you're on a Filling & Healthy day, so you can cook and eat it confident in the knowledge that you won't need to count anything.

Counting your daily allowance

If you are counting everything, you will see on the recipe exactly how many *ProPoints* values you will need to use from your *ProPoints* allowance. This makes it really easy to follow the plan while cooking from scratch as there is no guesswork involved.

Find out more at www.weightwatchers.co.uk

What exactly CAN I DO with 5 ProPoints values – or even FEWER?

The answer is in this book. Making the most of your precious **ProPoints** values is very important and dipping into these pages will give you plenty of inspiration and ideas. Start browsing now to find simple but delicious combinations for snacks, breakfasts, lunches, desserts and even hearty dinners.

The chapters are divided according to **ProPoints** values, from 0 to 5 – and all the recipes are straightforward, easy to follow, and use everyday ingredients.

If you are following the Filling & Healthy approach, there are plenty of dishes to choose from. We have even included an index of mix-and-match serving suggestions, so if you are feeling really hungry you can add extras but still keep on track.

WHEN WOULD I USE THIS BOOK?

It's not always easy to know how to maximise your **ProPoints** values. You might imagine that 5 **ProPoints** values are not quite enough for a full meal. Or perhaps you think there won't be any recipes that you fancy making. Well, read on!

It's the weekend: I've had brunch. I'm out for dinner but just need a snack to keep me going…

Then try one of the tasty rice cake toppers, perhaps Broad Bean and Parma Ham or Chilli Chicken, for 3 **ProPoints** values. Or if you want something sweet and satisfying, try Honeyed Tropical Fruit Salad for only 1 **ProPoints** value.

I'm having a bad day and I need to get back on track: what can I have for dinner?

Try quick and tasty Spring Veg Spaghetti for only 5 **ProPoints** values or filling Chunky Sausage and Bean Casserole for just 4 **ProPoints** values.

I need to be out of the house in 30 minutes. I'll just have a couple of chocolate biscuits…

Stop! How about Lunchbox Chickpea Dip, ready in a flash? Serve it with a mound of crudités for just 4 **ProPoints** values. Or put together a Delicious Blue Cheese and Pear Salad, fast and tasty – and still only 3 **ProPoints** values.

I've got a really busy week coming up. what can I prepare ahead?

Chicken and Barley Stew freezes well and can be defrosted overnight and reheated in a pan or microwave. Batch cook the Simple Tomato Sauce: it'll save you time when you prepare Mediterranean Haddock – or simply serve it with pasta.

Veggie friends are coming for lunch. I want to cook them something delicious but need to keep the ProPoints values low…

May we suggest Favourite Cheesy Stuffed Mushrooms followed by Apple and Pear Brown Betty? That's a lovely two-course lunch for 6 **ProPoints** values. Who wouldn't be impressed!

Five & Under will not only help keep you on track, it will continue to inspire you and help you to be creative with your food choices. It's your life, so go on, enjoy it – and enjoy cooking!

Accompaniments GUIDE

Accompaniment	Portion size	ProPoints values
Bread, white	35 g (1¼ oz) slice	2
Bread, wholemeal	35 g (1¼ oz) slice	2
Bulgur wheat, cooked	80 g (3 oz)	2
Bulgur wheat, dried	60 g (2 oz)	5
Couscous, cooked	110 g (4 oz)	3
Couscous, dried	30 g (1¼ oz)	3
Couscous, wholewheat, cooked	90 g (3¼ oz)	3
Couscous, wholewheat, dried	30 g (1¼ oz)	3
Crumpet, Weight Watchers	37 g each	2
Naan bread	70 g (2½ oz)	6
Noodles, egg, cooked	100 g (3½ oz)	4
Noodles, egg, dried	40 g (1½ oz)	4
Noodles, rice, dried	40 g (1½ oz)	4
Noodles, rice, ready cooked	150 g (5½ oz)	4
Pasta, white, cooked	150 g (5½ oz)	4
Pasta, white, dried	40 g (1½ oz)	4
Pasta, wholewheat, cooked	130 g (4½ oz)	4
Pasta, wholewheat, dried	40 g (1½ oz)	4
Potato, baked	100 g (3½ oz)	4
Potato wedges (oven ready, Co-operative)	150 g (5½ oz)	5
Potatoes, raw or boiled or mashed (without added ingredients)	100 g (3½ oz)	2
Potatoes, roast (oven ready, Sainsbury's)	130 g (4½ oz)	4
Quinoa, cooked	160 g (5¾ oz)	5
Quinoa, dried	60 g (2 oz)	5
Rice, brown, cooked	75 g (2¾ oz)	3
Rice, brown, dried	30 g (1¼ oz)	3
Rice, white, cooked	75 g (2¾ oz)	3
Rice, white, dried	30 g (1¼ oz)	3
Tortilla wrap, Weight Watchers	42 g each	3

Quick ProPoints VALUES index

Curried cauliflower soup **12**

Spring vegetable stew **14**

Mexican slaw **16**

Fennel roasted peppers **18**

Fresh vegetable pho **20**

Moroccan carrot salad **22**

Butternut and cauliflower cakes **24**

Simple tomato sauce **26**

Strawberry and banana sorbet **28**

Winter vegetable curry **32**

Super tasty sauces **34**

Creamy roasted tomato soup **36**

Really quick hot Thai prawns **38**

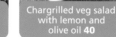

Chargrilled veg salad with lemon and olive oil **40**

Easy apple Waldorf **42**

Honeyed tropical fruit salad **44**

Gorgeous roasted roots **48**

A simple tomato omelette **50**

Bacon and butternut bubble and squeak **52**

Apple and pear brown Betty **54**

Almond oats brekkie
58

The cooked breakfast
60

Creamy mushrooms
on toast 62

The nicest toppers
64

Delicious blue cheese
and pear salad 66

Quick chicken and
mango salad 68

Scrumptious chorizo
tomatoes with eggs
70

Honey poached
plums 72

Seven-minute naan
76

Lunchbox chickpea
dip 78

Leek and potato
patties 80

Favourite cheesy
stuffed mushrooms
82

Chicken and barley
stew 84

Fabulous oregano
pork and ratatouille
bake 86

Chunky sausage and
bean casserole 88

Summer fruits
Eton mess 90

Spring veg spaghetti
94

Baked aubergine and
halloumi parcels 96

Loaded veggie nachos
98

Chilli prawn stir-fry
100

Mediterranean
haddock 102

Smoky chicken in a pot
104

The best turkey burgers
106

Red lentil dhal
108

Sliced marinated steak
and salad 110

QUICK *PROPOINTS* VALUES INDEX *Five & Under* 9

Zero ProPoints values

Curried *Cauliflower* Soup

0 *ProPoints* values per serving
ProPoints values per recipe 2

Serves 4
Preparation time: 10 minutes

Cooking time: 20 minutes

calorie controlled cooking spray
2 onions, chopped
1 tablespoon medium curry powder
1 small cauliflower, chopped
 (include stem and leaves for
 extra flavour)
850 ml (1½ pints) vegetable stock
1 bay leaf
1 teaspoon cumin seeds
salt and freshly ground black
 pepper
a handful of fresh coriander leaves,
 to garnish

Cauliflower makes a robust, satisfying and delicious soup, especially when it's given a spicy flavour boost.

Heat a large lidded saucepan and mist with the cooking spray. Add the onions and cook, stirring, for 4 minutes, until softened, adding a little water if the onions begin to stick. Add the curry powder and cauliflower pieces and stir-fry for 1 minute.

Pour over the stock, add the bay leaf and bring to the boil; reduce the heat and cover the pan. Simmer gently for 15 minutes until the cauliflower is tender. Dry-fry the cumin seeds for a minute or so in a small pan, until you can smell the aroma.

Remove the bay leaf, transfer the soup to a blender (or use a hand-held blender) and blitz until smooth. Return the soup to the pan and warm through. Season and serve garnished with the cumin seeds and coriander leaves.

Variation

For a creamy version, add 100 ml (3½ fl oz) reduced fat coconut milk and reduce the stock to 700 ml (1¼ pints) for an additional 1 *ProPoints* value.

Spring VEGETABLE Stew

 ProPoints values per serving
ProPoints values per recipe 1

 Serves 4
Takes 25 minutes

 calorie controlled cooking spray
8 baby onions or shallots, peeled
    and halved
3 carrots, chopped
400 g can artichoke hearts, drained
    and halved
700 ml (1¼ pints) vegetable stock
200 g (7 oz) broccoli florets
2 tablespoons chopped fresh
    tarragon
salt and freshly ground black
    pepper

This really easy stew is quick to prepare and makes a great lunch – or serve it with garlic toast (see Cook's tip, page 20) for supper.

Heat a large lidded pan and mist with the cooking spray. Add the onions or shallots and cook over a low heat for 4–5 minutes, stirring them occasionally so that they soften but don't catch. Add the carrots, artichoke hearts and stock. Bring to the boil, reduce the heat, cover and simmer for 5 minutes.

Stir in the broccoli and half the tarragon and cook for a further 3–4 minutes until everything is just tender. Season and serve in warm bowls with the remaining tarragon sprinkled over.

Mexican
Slaw

 ProPoints values per serving
ProPoints values per recipe 2

 Serves 2
Takes 15 minutes

100 g (3½ oz) red cabbage,
   shredded finely
1 carrot, grated
½ fennel bulb, sliced thinly
3 radishes, sliced thinly
zest and juice of ½ lime
½ green chilli, diced
a small handful of fresh coriander
   leaves, torn
salt and freshly ground black
   pepper

Shop-bought coleslaw is usually heavily laden with mayonnaise, but with this home-made crunchy version you can eat a lot more for fewer *ProPoints* values.

Combine all the ingredients, then cover and chill until required.

Cook's tips Toss in 20 g (¾ oz) toasted pine nut kernels just before serving for an extra 2 *ProPoints* values.

The slaw goes well with the Really Quick Hot Thai Prawns on page 38. It is also a good accompaniment to the Loaded Veggie Nachos on page 98.

Fennel Roasted PEPPERS

 ProPoints values per serving
ProPoints values per recipe 1

 Serves 2
Preparation time: 10 minutes

 Cooking time: 30 minutes

2 red peppers, halved and
   de-seeded
1 fennel bulb, cut into thin wedges
8 cherry tomatoes
1 red onion, cut into thin wedges
4 garlic cloves
calorie controlled cooking spray
2 sprigs of fresh thyme
1 tablespoon balsamic vinegar
salt and freshly ground black
   pepper
a handful of rocket, to serve
   (optional)

Roasting the peppers gives them lovely caramelised edges that complement the tomatoes and the balsamic dressing in this delicious vegetarian dish.

Preheat the oven to Gas Mark 6/200°C/fan oven 180°C. Place the peppers, fennel, tomatoes, onion and garlic in a roasting tray and spray with the cooking spray. Scatter with the thyme and seasoning and roast for 30 minutes until the vegetables are softened and beginning to char.

Remove the garlic cloves and squeeze out the flesh, discarding the papery skin. Combine the soft garlic with the balsamic vinegar.

Fill the pepper halves with the vegetables and serve drizzled with the balsamic dressing and some rocket leaves, if using.

Cook's tip For an extra 3 **ProPoints** values serve the peppers with lemon couscous: 60 g (2 oz) dried couscous soaked in 200 ml (7 fl oz) vegetable stock with the zest of a lemon stirred through.

Fresh *Vegetable* Pho

 ProPoints values per serving
ProPoints values per recipe 0

 Serves 1
Takes 15 minutes

 200 ml (7 fl oz) vegetable stock
2 cm (¾ inch) piece fresh root
    ginger, peeled and cut into
    matchsticks
½ teaspoon finely chopped red
    chilli, plus extra to garnish
    (optional)
1 teaspoon lime juice
a good handful of beansprouts
a good handful of mange tout
3 baby corn, halved
salt and freshly ground black
    pepper
1 tablespoon torn fresh mint leaves
1 tablespoon torn fresh coriander
    leaves

You can use whatever zero *ProPoints* value vegetables you have to hand for this dish — even leftover cooked vegetables such as carrots or cabbage.

Bring the stock to the boil, add the ginger, chilli and lime juice, and simmer gently for 5 minutes to allow the flavours to infuse.

Add the beansprouts, mange tout and corn, bring back to the boil and simmer for 2–3 minutes until just tender. Ladle into a bowl, season and top with the mint and coriander, and extra chilli if using.

Cook's tips Add 150 g (5½ oz) straight-to-wok noodles with the vegetables for an extra 6 *ProPoints* values.

Serve with garlic toast: a Weight Watchers brown bread slice, toasted and rubbed with a cut garlic clove, for an extra 1 *ProPoints* value.

Make a batch of stock and freeze it in portions ready to add vegetables.

Moroccan CARROT
Salad

 ProPoints values per serving
ProPoints values per recipe 1

 Serves 4
Preparation time: 10 minutes
Cooking time: 10 minutes

 ½ teaspoon ground ginger
1 teaspoon ground coriander
½ teaspoon ground cumin
½ teaspoon ground cinnamon
250 ml (9 fl oz) vegetable stock
400 g (14 oz) carrots, sliced
calorie controlled cooking spray
1 red onion, sliced
1 small green chilli, chopped finely
2 garlic cloves, chopped
salt and freshly ground black
    pepper

This makes a great side dish for a simple grilled steak or chicken breast. The carrots absorb all the flavour of the spices as they cook.

Dry-fry the spices in a medium lidded pan for a minute or so until you can smell the aroma. Add the stock and carrots and bring to the boil. Reduce the heat, cover and simmer for 10 minutes until tender.

Heat a frying pan and mist with the cooking spray. Add the onion, chilli and garlic and stir-fry gently for around 8 minutes, adding a little water if necessary, until softened.

Add the carrots to the frying pan with any remaining cooking liquid and toss through. Season. Serve warm or set aside to cool.

Cook's tip This salad keeps well, covered, in the fridge for up to 2 days.

BUTTERNUT & Cauliflower Cakes

 ProPoints values per serving
ProPoints values per recipe 0

 Serves 4
Takes 30 minutes

 400 g (14 oz) butternut squash,
   peeled and chopped
200 g (7 oz) cauliflower florets
4 sprigs of fresh thyme, leaves only
2 tablespoons chopped fresh parsley
1 tablespoon ground coriander
calorie controlled cooking spray
salt and freshly ground black
   pepper

For the salsa
2 tomatoes, de-seeded and cubed
2 spring onions, sliced finely
a handful of fresh coriander leaves,
   torn
a squeeze of lemon juice

These delicious vegetable cakes make a great light lunch or are perfect for when you're just in the door in the evening – simply prepare ahead and then all you need to do is mash and cook.

Combine the salsa ingredients and set aside.

Place the butternut squash and cauliflower florets in a steamer or colander over a large pan of water. Bring to the boil and steam for 10–12 minutes until soft. Tip them into a large bowl.

Mash the cooked vegetables until smooth. Add the thyme, parsley, coriander, salt to taste and plenty of freshly ground black pepper, and mix well.

Heat a non-stick frying pan and mist with the cooking spray. Add a large spoonful of the mixture and cook, turning regularly, for 3–4 minutes until golden – you may need to do this in batches. Serve 2 cakes per person with the salsa alongside.

Cook's tip A 125 g (4½ oz) lean pork shoulder steak is a great partner: grill for 10 minutes, turning regularly, until cooked through, for an extra 4 *ProPoints* values.

Simple
TOMATO Sauce

 ProPoints values per serving
ProPoints values per recipe 1

 Serves 4
Preparation time: 5 minutes
Cooking time: 30 minutes

 calorie controlled cooking spray
1 large onion, chopped
1 garlic clove, crushed
400 g can chopped tomatoes
1 tablespoon tomato purée
1 vegetable stock cube, dissolved in
    150 ml (5 fl oz) hot water
salt and freshly ground black
    pepper

This sauce can form the basis for many a dish: serve it as is with cooked pasta or grilled meat and fish, or experiment with our variations below.

Heat a medium pan and mist with the cooking spray. Add the onion and cook gently for 10 minutes, adding a little water if it begins to stick. Add the garlic and cook for a further minute.

Add the tomatoes, tomato purée, stock and seasoning. Bring to the boil, then reduce the heat and simmer gently for 20 minutes.

Variations

Hot tomato sauce: add ½ teaspoon chilli powder with the garlic.

Herby tomato sauce: add 1 teaspoon mixed dried herbs with the garlic, or stir through a handful of mixed fresh herbs such as basil, parsley and oregano just before serving.

Vegetable and tomato sauce: add 200 g (7 oz) sliced mushrooms or 1 large red pepper, chopped, when you add the onion.

Cook's tip Use the basic sauce to make Baked Aubergine and Halloumi Parcels on page 96 and Mediterranean Haddock on page 102.

Strawberry & BANANA Sorbet

 0 *ProPoints* values per serving
ProPoints values per recipe 0

 Serves 2
Takes 10 minutes + freezing

 2 bananas

 6 large strawberries, hulled and
chopped
1 teaspoon finely grated orange
zest
juice of ½ orange

Freeze the bananas in advance and then all you have to do is blend it all together to make this delicious fruity ice.

Place the whole bananas in their skins in the freezer for 24 hours.

Remove the bananas from the freezer, peel and place in a liquidiser (or use a hand-held blender) and blend with the strawberries, orange zest and juice. Serve immediately or spoon into freezerproof ramekins and freeze until required.

Cook's tip If you are serving the sorbet from frozen, remove it from the freezer 10 minutes beforehand, to allow it to soften.

One
ProPoints
value

Winter VEGETABLE Curry

 ProPoints value per serving
ProPoints values per recipe 3

 Serves 4
Preparation time: 10 minutes
Cooking time: 35–40 minutes

 2 tablespoons hot curry powder
250 g (9 oz) butternut squash,
    peeled and cubed
2 carrots, chopped
½ small swede, peeled and cubed
calorie controlled cooking spray
2 x 400 g cans chopped tomatoes
400 ml (14 fl oz) vegetable stock
salt and freshly ground black
    pepper
fresh coriander leaves, to garnish
60 g (2 oz) 0% fat natural Greek
    yogurt, to serve

Curries often taste better the following day, so if you can make this and resist eating it for 24 hours the flavours will develop nicely.

Dry-fry the curry powder in a large lidded pan for 30 seconds. Add the butternut squash, carrots and swede, mist with the cooking spray and toss to coat. Add the tomatoes, stock and seasoning, bring to the boil, cover and simmer for 35–40 minutes until the vegetables are tender.

Serve in large bowls, garnished with coriander leaves, and stir in some of the cooling yogurt.

Cook's tip Serve with a 60 g (2 oz) portion of basmati rice per person, cooked according to the packet instructions, for an extra 6 **ProPoints** values each. Or try making the Seven-minute Naan on page 76 for an extra 4 **ProPoints** values per naan.

SUPER **TASTY** SAUCES

Here's what you can do with a pot of 0% fat natural Greek yogurt...

To serve with **Steak** *(top left)*

1 ProPoints value per serving
ProPoints values per recipe 2

V Serves 4
Takes 5 minutes

Combine a 150 g pot of 0% fat natural Greek yogurt with 2 teaspoons of grainy mustard, ½ teaspoon of horseradish sauce and a large handful of fresh flat leaf parsley, chopped. Season with a little salt and freshly ground black pepper. Add a splash of warm water to make the sauce runnier if you prefer.

To serve with **Grilled Fish** *(top right)*

1 ProPoints value per serving
ProPoints values per recipe 3

V Serves 4
Takes 5 minutes

Combine a 150 g pot of 0% fat natural Greek yogurt with 1 tablespoon of reduced fat mayonnaise, 1 tablespoon of chopped capers, ½ teaspoon of lemon zest and 2 teaspoons each of chopped fresh dill and chives. Season with a little salt and freshly ground black pepper.

To serve with **Chicken** *(bottom right)*

1 ProPoints value per serving
ProPoints values per recipe 2

V Serves 4
Takes 5 minutes

Mist a small pan with calorie controlled cooking spray, add 2 finely sliced shallots and sauté until soft, adding a little water if they stick. Remove from the heat. Stir in a small handful of chopped fresh tarragon and ½ teaspoon of lemon or orange zest, with a 150 g pot of 0% fat natural Greek yogurt, and season with a little salt and freshly ground black pepper.

To serve with **Prawns** *(bottom left)*

1 ProPoints value per serving
ProPoints values per recipe 3

Serves 4
Takes 5 minutes

Combine a 150 g pot of 0% fat natural Greek yogurt with 1 tablespoon of tomato ketchup, 2 teaspoons of tomato purée and a dash of Worcestershire sauce, then season with a little salt and freshly ground black pepper.

Creamy Roasted TOMATO Soup

ProPoints value per serving
ProPoints values per recipe 3

Serves 2
Preparation time: 5 minutes
Cooking time: 40 minutes

400 g (14 oz) vine tomatoes, halved
1 large onion, sliced
4 garlic cloves
calorie controlled cooking spray
2 sprigs of fresh rosemary
600 ml (20 fl oz) hot vegetable stock
½ teaspoon sweetener
100 g (3½ oz) quark
1 tablespoon snipped fresh chives,
  plus extra to garnish
salt and freshly ground black
  pepper

Roasting the vegetables in this soup intensifies the flavour. Try adding a pinch of chilli flakes with the rosemary if you like things spicy.

Preheat the oven to Gas Mark 7/220°C/fan oven 200°C. Place the tomatoes, onion and garlic cloves in a roasting tray in a single layer. Mist with the cooking spray and lay the rosemary on top. Cook for 30–35 minutes until the onion has softened.

Bring the stock to the boil in a large pan. Squeeze the garlic flesh from the skin and add it to the pan along with the rest of the roasted vegetables. Bring up to the boil again and simmer for a minute until hot. Remove from the heat and use a hand-held blender to blend the soup. Add the sweetener and half the quark and blend again. Pass the soup through a sieve to remove the tomato seeds, then season.

Combine the remaining quark with the chives and 1 tablespoon of water to give a runny consistency, and swirl into the soup. Sprinkle with the extra chives and some black pepper.

Cook's tip Add a 20 g (¾ oz) slice of French stick for an extra 1 **ProPoints** value.

Really Quick *Hot* THAI *Prawns*

 ProPoints value per serving
ProPoints values per recipe 2

 Serves 2
Takes 8 minutes

1 fresh lemongrass stalk, chopped
    finely
½ red chilli, de-seeded and cubed
finely grated zest and juice of 1 lime
a splash of Thai fish sauce
2 spring onions, sliced
1 small carrot, grated
8 cherry tomatoes, halved
100 g (3½ oz) cooked, peeled
    prawns
4 Sweet Gem lettuce leaves
a handful of fresh coriander leaves,
    to garnish (optional)
salt and freshly ground black
    pepper

Lemongrass and lime add a wonderful fragrant note to this fresh warm salad dish.

Combine the lemongrass with the red chilli, lime zest and juice and fish sauce in a small pan. Warm gently, then add the spring onions, carrot, tomatoes and prawns. Stir to coat and warm through. Season to taste.

Arrange the lettuce leaves on 2 plates. Fill them with the prawn mixture and scatter with the coriander leaves, if using.

Cook's tip This is equally good served warm or chilled in the fridge for a couple of hours. Add a 40 g (1½ oz) portion of brown rice, cooked according to the packet instructions, to each serving for an extra 4 *ProPoints* values.

Chargrilled VEG SALAD
with *Lemon* & Olive Oil

 1 *ProPoints* value per serving
ProPoints values per recipe 3

 Serves 2
Preparation time: 10 minutes
Cooking time: 10–15 minutes

calorie controlled cooking spray
8 spring onions, trimmed
½ red pepper, cut into strips
½ yellow pepper, cut into strips
1 small fennel bulb, sliced thinly
6 asparagus spears, halved if long
finely grated zest and juice of
    ½ lemon
2 teaspoons extra virgin olive oil
a handful of fresh mint leaves, torn
a handful of fresh basil leaves, torn
sea salt and freshly ground black
    pepper

The key to cooking vegetables on a griddle pan is to slice them thinly and evenly, and spray them generously with the calorie controlled cooking spray before you start.

Heat the griddle pan until smoking. Spray the vegetables generously with the cooking spray and cook in batches, turning once during cooking, then set aside. If you want to serve them warm, cover and place in a low oven.

Arrange the vegetables on a serving platter. Combine the lemon zest and juice with the olive oil. Scatter the herbs over the vegetables and season with some sea salt and black pepper, then drizzle with the dressing. You can chill the salad in the fridge and enjoy it later, or serve it warm straightaway.

Easy *Apple* WALDORF

 1 *ProPoints* value per serving
ProPoints values per recipe 5

 Serves 4
Takes 10 minutes

125 g (4½ oz) white cabbage,
shredded
1 small red onion, sliced finely
1 red apple, cored and chopped
2 celery sticks, chopped
2 tablespoons fat-free dressing
25 g (1 oz) walnuts, chopped
salt and freshly ground black
pepper

This is a lovely crunchy lunch on its own — or try it with The Best Turkey Burgers on page 106. Toasting the nuts really enhances their flavour.

Combine the cabbage, onion, apple and celery in a large bowl. Toss with the dressing and seasoning.

Dry-fry the walnuts in a small frying pan for a minute until toasted and sprinkle them over the salad.

Honeyed *Tropical* FRUIT Salad

 ProPoints value per serving
ProPoints values per recipe 1

 Serves 2
Takes 10 minutes

1 small ripe mango, cubed
1 small papaya, peeled, halved,
   de-seeded and sliced
1 kiwi, peeled, sliced and halved
1 passion fruit
juice of 1 lime
2 teaspoons clear honey

Fresh, tangy and versatile — you could serve this for breakfast, as a snack or for dessert.

Arrange the mango, papaya and kiwi on 2 small plates.

Halve the passion fruit and scoop out the seeds and juice into a bowl. Stir in the lime juice and honey. Drizzle over the fruit and serve.

> *Cook's tip* Serve each portion with:
>
> 100 g (3½ oz) 0% fat natural Greek yogurt for 1 extra *ProPoints* value per serving.
>
> 2 x 10 g (¼ oz) ginger snap biscuits crumbled over, for an extra 2 *ProPoints* values per serving.
>
> 60 g (2 oz) scoop of low fat vanilla ice cream for an additional 2 *ProPoints* values per serving.

Two
ProPoints
values

Gorgeous ROASTED Roots

 2 *ProPoints* values per serving
ProPoints values per recipe 5

Serves 2
Preparation time: 10 minutes
Cooking time: 30 minutes

1 parsnip, peeled and cut into
   chunks
2 large carrots, cut into chunks
2 beetroot, trimmed and cut into
   wedges
2 teaspoons garam masala
2 teaspoons olive oil
sea salt and freshly ground black
   pepper

Tender roasted vegetables with a hint of spice make a great side dish or a light vegetarian lunch.

Preheat the oven to Gas Mark 6/200°C/fan oven 180°C.

Arrange the root vegetables in a roasting tin large enough to hold them in a single layer. Mix the garam masala with a tablespoon of water to make a thin paste, then spoon it over the vegetables. Drizzle with the oil and toss so that everything is evenly coated. Sprinkle with a little sea salt and some black pepper and roast for 30 minutes until tender and beginning to char.

Cook's tips Delicious as a side dish with a grilled-to-your-liking 225 g (8 oz) lean sirloin steak, for an additional 7 *ProPoints* values.

Serve with a zero *ProPoints* value green salad if you like.

A Simple TOMATO
Omelette

 ProPoints values per serving
ProPoints values per recipe 2

 Serves 1
Preparation time: 5 minutes
 Cooking time: 10 minutes

calorie controlled cooking spray
½ red pepper, cut into thin strips
1 small onion, sliced thinly
1 egg, beaten
1 egg white
1 teaspoon snipped fresh chives
1 tomato, sliced
salt and freshly ground black
    pepper

This is a quick, satisfying lunch or breakfast for one.

Heat a medium non-stick frying pan and mist with the cooking spray. Add the pepper and onion and stir-fry over a medium heat for 5–6 minutes until softened – if the mixture begins to stick, just add a little water.

Beat together the egg and egg white, season, and stir in the chives. Increase the heat under the frying pan and add the egg mixture, swirling round the pan to reach the sides. Top with the tomato slices and cook for 2–3 minutes until the omelette is just set on top and golden underneath.

Flip in half and slide from the pan on to a serving plate.

Variation
Fancy a meaty version? Add 2 chopped bacon medallions to cook with the vegetables for 1 extra **ProPoints** value.

Cook's tip Serve with a zero *ProPoints* value green salad if you like.

Bacon & BUTTERNUT
Bubble & Squeak

 ProPoints values per serving
ProPoints values per recipe 4

 Serves 2
Takes 15 minutes

1 teaspoon olive oil
250 g (9 oz) butternut squash, peeled and cubed
4 bacon medallions, cut into strips
100 g (3½ oz) cabbage, shredded
4 spring onions, sliced
6 cherry tomatoes, halved
salt and freshly ground black pepper
1 tablespoon grainy mustard, to serve

This is a great way to use up leftover cooked vegetables and can be served as an accompaniment or light lunch.

Heat the oil in a non-stick lidded frying pan and when hot add the butternut squash. Stir-fry for 5 minutes. Add a splash of water, cover and cook for 2 minutes until tender.

Add the bacon, cabbage and spring onions and continue cooking for 2–3 minutes until the bacon is cooked. Season with a little salt and freshly ground black pepper.

Stir in the cherry tomatoes and mix through until just warm. Serve with mustard on the side.

Variation
Make this into a hearty brunch by adding a poached egg on top for an extra 2 *ProPoints* values.

Cook's tip Both the butternut squash and cabbage could be precooked and simply added to the pan to heat through.

APPLE & Pear BROWN BETTY

 ProPoints values per serving
ProPoints values per recipe 8

 Serves 4
Takes 25 minutes

2 large eating apples, peeled,
cored and chopped

3 ripe pears, peeled, cored and
chopped

20 g (¾ oz) low fat spread

75 g (2¾ oz) fresh brown
breadcrumbs

3 teaspoons dark brown sugar

1 teaspoon cinnamon

Brown Betty is a traditional American dessert of sweetened crumbs with cooked fruits. This version uses apples and pears for their natural sweetness.

Place the apples and pears in a medium pan with 2 tablespoons of water and simmer gently for 10 minutes until softened. Remove from the heat.

Melt the low fat spread in a non-stick frying pan, add the breadcrumbs, sugar and cinnamon and cook, stirring regularly, over a medium heat for 3–4 minutes until crispy.

Spoon the cooked fruit into serving glasses or ramekins and top with the breadcrumb mixture. Serve warm, or cool and chill until required.

Variation
Try adding a handful of fresh berries in place of one of the pears.

Three ProPoints values

ALMOND
Oats Brekkie

Serves 1
Takes 5 minutes + overnight soaking

25 g (1 oz) porridge oats
100 ml (3½ fl oz) unsweetened almond milk
1 apple, cored and grated
a handful of raspberries

Start making this satisfying breakfast the night before, to allow the almond milk to soak into the oats.

Place the oats and milk in a serving bowl, stir to combine, then cover and refrigerate until morning.

Stir in the remaining ingredients and serve.

Cook's tip The oats and almond milk mixture will keep covered in the fridge for up to 2 days.

The COOKED Breakfast

 3 *ProPoints* values per serving
ProPoints values per recipe 3

 Serves 1
Takes 10 minutes

2 bacon medallions
4 mushrooms
1 tomato, halved
calorie controlled cooking spray
1 egg

Don't just save it for mornings — you can enjoy a cooked breakfast at any time of day...

Preheat the grill to medium and line a grill pan with foil. Place the bacon, mushrooms and tomato on the foil and mist with the cooking spray. Grill for 5 minutes until cooked.

In the meantime, heat a small non-stick frying pan and mist with the cooking spray. Crack the egg into a ramekin then add to the pan – this helps the egg to keep its shape. Cook for 2–3 minutes until the white is just set.

Serve the breakfast on a warm plate.

Cook's tips Add a Weight Watchers Cumberland sausage for an extra 1 *ProPoints* value.

Serve with a crumpet for an extra 2 *ProPoints* values.

Creamy MUSHROOMS on Toast

Serves 1
Takes 10 minutes

calorie controlled cooking spray
200 g (7 oz) mushrooms, sliced if
    large
1 small garlic clove, crushed
4 tablespoons vegetable stock
25 g (1 oz) quark
2 x 20 g (¾ oz) slices calorie
    controlled brown bread
salt and freshly ground black
    pepper
chopped fresh parsley, to garnish

Mushrooms are really good at absorbing flavours and go very well with garlic. Adding a little stock creates tasty juices to soak into the toast.

Heat a small non-stick frying pan until hot, mist with the cooking spray and add the mushrooms and garlic. Cook for 3–4 minutes, then add the stock and continue cooking for around 2 minutes until the mushrooms are soft and juicy. Stir in the quark and warm through. Season with a little salt and freshly ground black pepper.

Toast the bread under the grill until golden. Serve the mushrooms on top with a sprinkling of parsley.

The NICEST Toppers

ProPoints values per serving

ProPoints values per recipe 3

Each recipe serves 1
Each recipe takes 5 minutes

These deliciously easy toppers can be made in minutes or prepared in the morning to take to work. Pack the rice cakes separately and assemble at the last minute to stop them from going soft.

Broad Bean & Parma Ham *(top left)*

50 g (1¾ oz) frozen broad beans, defrosted in hot water • a squeeze of lemon juice • 1 rice cake • a few sprigs of watercress • 1 slice Parma ham • salt and freshly ground black pepper

Drain the beans and slip them out of their skins. Discard the skins. The beans should now weigh 30 g (1¼ oz). Crush the beans roughly using the back of a fork. Stir in the lemon juice and seasoning. Serve on top of the rice cake with the watercress and slice of Parma ham.

Cook's tip Dry-fry or grill the Parma ham and crumble it over the beans for a more intense flavour.

Ⓥ Pea & Mint *(top right)*

60 g (2 oz) frozen peas, defrosted in hot water • 1 tablespoon quark • 1 Little Gem lettuce leaf, torn • a couple of fresh mint leaves, plus extra to garnish • 1 rice cake • salt and freshly ground black pepper

Drain the peas and place all the ingredients for the topping in a mini blender and blend roughly. Season to taste. Top the rice cake and garnish with extra mint.

Italian Style *(bottom right)*

1 rice cake • 30 g (1¼ oz) light mozzarella, sliced • 1 tomato, sliced • a few fresh basil leaves • 2 teaspoons red pesto • salt and freshly ground black pepper

Top the rice cake with the mozzarella, tomato and basil. Season then drizzle the pesto over the top.

Chilli Chicken *(bottom left)*

30 g (1¼ oz) cooked skinless, boneless chicken breast, torn into pieces • 1 tablespoon sweet chilli sauce • 1 rice cake • salt and freshly ground black pepper • a handful of rocket

Combine the chicken and chilli sauce, season and use to top the rice cake. Serve with the rocket.

Delicious Blue Cheese & PEAR Salad

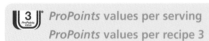 *ProPoints* values per serving
ProPoints values per recipe 3

Serves 1
Takes 5 minutes

1 Little Gem lettuce heart, shredded
a handful of watercress
1 small ripe pear, sliced thinly
a squeeze of lemon juice
30 g (1¼ oz) Danish blue or
    Roquefort cheese, crumbled or
    sliced thinly
a handful of pomegranate seeds

This is a really simple yet winning combination.

Arrange the salad leaves on a serving plate. Toss the pear with the lemon juice and add to the salad leaves. Top with the cheese and pomegranate seeds.

Cook's tip Serve with a 40 g (1½ oz) slice soda bread for an extra 2 *ProPoints* values.

Quick *Chicken* & MANGO Salad

 3 *ProPoints* values per serving
ProPoints values per recipe 6

 Serves 2
Preparation time: 15 minutes
Cooking time: 10 minutes

2 x 125 g (4½ oz) skinless, boneless
    chicken breasts
calorie controlled cooking spray
1 large courgette, cut into ribbons
1 large carrot, cut into ribbons
2 large handfuls of rocket or
    watercress
salt and freshly ground black
    pepper

For the salsa and dressing
1 small mango
½ small red onion, cubed
6 cherry tomatoes, quartered
a handful of fresh coriander leaves
a squeeze of lime juice

The mango dressing adds a lovely sweet and sour flavour to this warm salad.

Make the salsa and dressing. Peel the mango: cube half finely and combine with the red onion, tomatoes and coriander. Roughly chop the remainder and blitz in a food processor, adding a little lime juice to create a runny dressing. Season with a pinch of salt.

Place the chicken breasts between 2 sheets of cling film and bash with the end of a rolling pin to flatten them. Season and mist with the cooking spray.

Heat a griddle pan until smoking. Add the chicken breasts and cook for 5–7 minutes, turning, until golden and cooked through. Cut into slices, set aside and keep warm.

Mist the courgette ribbons with the cooking spray and cook quickly until just marked on both sides.

Combine the courgette, carrot and rocket or watercress and divide between 2 serving plates. Top with the chicken strips and some salsa, and drizzle the dressing over the top.

Cook's tip Serve with wholewheat couscous if you're extra hungry: cook 60 g (2 oz) dried weight per portion for an extra 6 *ProPoints* values.

Scrumptious
Chorizo Tomatoes with EGGS

 3 *ProPoints* values per serving
ProPoints values per recipe 7

Serves 2
Takes 15 minutes

calorie controlled cooking spray
1 onion, sliced
1 yellow pepper, chopped
4 tomatoes, chopped roughly
30 g (1¼ oz) chorizo, diced
2 eggs
salt and freshly ground black
   pepper
chopped fresh parsley, to garnish

Try serving these for a lazy weekend brunch or a really quick 'just in the door' dinner.

Heat a medium pan and mist with the cooking spray. Add the onion and pepper and stir-fry for 5–7 minutes until beginning to soften. If they start to stick, add a little water. Add the tomatoes and chorizo and continue cooking over a medium heat for 4–5 minutes until the tomatoes are beginning to break down. Season with salt and pepper.

Heat a non-stick frying pan and mist with the cooking spray. Crack the eggs one at a time into the pan and fry for 1–2 minutes until the white is just set.

Serve the chorizo mixture on plates with an egg on top, garnished with parsley.

Cook's tips Serve with a Weight Watchers tortilla for an extra 3 *ProPoints* values.

Stir in 200 g (7 oz) cooked new potatoes, cut into bite-size pieces, for the final 2 minutes of cooking time for an extra 2 *ProPoints* values.

Look out for spicy or picante chorizo if you enjoy hotness that comes from chilli.

Honey POACHED Plums

Serves 4
Take 15 minutes

8 plums, halved and stoned
6 teaspoons honey
2 star anise
4 x 60 g (2 oz) scoops low fat
    ice cream, to serve

You could cook these the day before, leaving the star anise in the syrup to infuse. Simply reheat gently in the pan if serving warm or keep for up to 3 days in the fridge and serve chilled.

Place the plums in a shallow lidded saucepan, add the honey and star anise with 100 ml (3½ fl oz) water. Bring to the boil, cover and reduce the heat to low. Cook for 8–10 minutes until the plums are tender but still keep their shape.

Set aside to cool. Serve warm or chilled with the ice cream.

Four
ProPoints
values

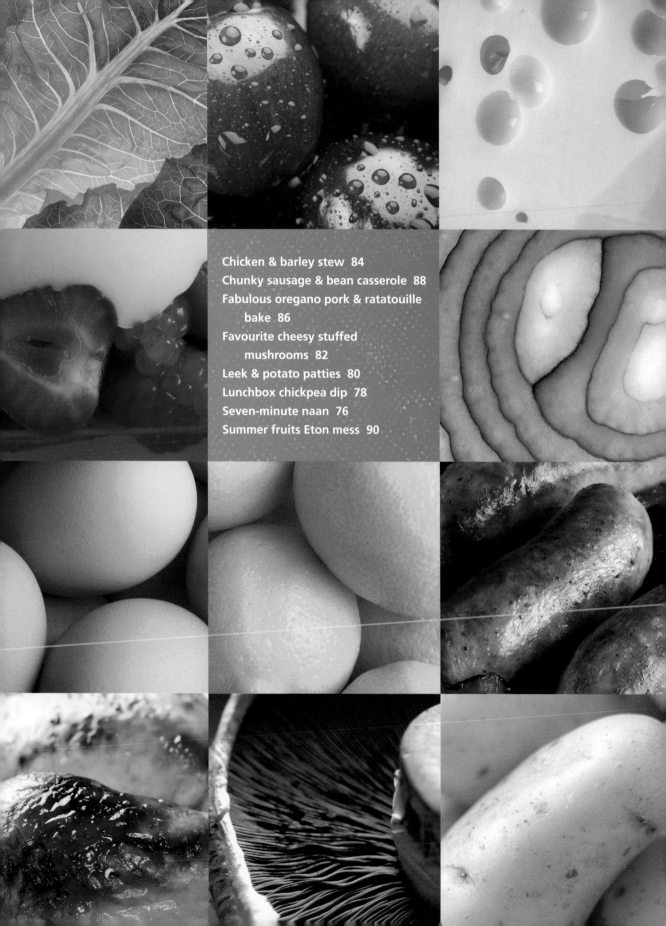

SEVEN-MINUTE Naan

ProPoints values per serving
ProPoints values per recipe 18

Makes 4 naans
Takes 7 minutes

200 g (7 oz) self-raising flour
2 teaspoons black onion seeds
around 125 ml (4 fl oz) sugar-free
  lemonade
calorie controlled cooking spray
salt and freshly ground black
  pepper

This is the most simple but delicious secret recipe for naan bread. Once you've made it, you'll never want to eat shop-bought again!

Sift the flour into a large bowl. Add a little salt, pepper and the onion seeds. Make a well in the middle and add enough lemonade to mix to a stiff, smooth dough. Shape into 4 rounds, each about 12 cm (4½ inches) in diameter.

Heat a small frying pan until hot, then mist with the cooking spray. Add one round of dough and cook for 1–2 minutes until puffed up and brown underneath. Mist the top side of the bread with the cooking spray, flip it over and cook for 1 minute. Serve warm.

Cook's tip Freeze the naan breads after cooking and cooling. Wrap them with greaseproof paper and place in freezer bags.

Lunchbox
CHICKPEA Dip

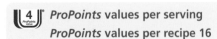 **ProPoints** values per serving
ProPoints values per recipe 16

V **Serves 4**
Takes 10 minutes

1 teaspoon ground cumin
400 g can chickpeas, drained
3 tablespoons tahini paste
1 garlic clove, crushed
a handful of fresh parsley, chopped
a squeeze of lemon juice
salt
carrot, celery and pepper sticks,
   to serve

Whizz this up and pack it in a pot for lunch, along with some crunchy vegetable sticks, or serve as a quick snack at home.

Sprinkle the cumin in a small pan or frying pan and dry-fry for a minute or so until you can smell the aroma.

Place the chickpeas, tahini and garlic in a mini blender and blitz to a paste. Add the cumin, parsley, some lemon juice and a little salt. Blend briefly and taste, adding more lemon or salt as required.

Serve with the vegetable sticks for dipping.

Leek & POTATO
Patties

ProPoints values per serving 4
ProPoints values per recipe 7

Serves 2
Takes 20 minutes

125 g (4½ oz) potatoes, chopped
calorie controlled cooking spray
1 large leek, sliced thinly
2 eggs
1 tablespoon snipped fresh chives
salt and freshly ground black
    pepper

For the dressing
1 tablespoon fat-free dressing
1 teaspoon grainy mustard

Try serving these for a lazy weekend brunch.

Make the dressing by combining the fat-free dressing and mustard, and set aside.

Bring a pan of water to the boil, add the potatoes and cook for 10–15 minutes until tender. Drain well and mash. Season.

While the potatoes are cooking, heat a lidded pan and mist with the cooking spray. Add the leek and stir-fry for 3 minutes, then add a splash of water, cover and cook for around 10 minutes until cooked through. Stir into the mash and mix well.

When cool enough to handle, shape the mixture into 4 rounds. Heat a non-stick frying pan and mist with the cooking spray. Add the patties and cook for 2–3 minutes, turning, until golden brown on both sides.

Bring a shallow lidded pan of water to the boil. Crack the eggs into a ramekin, one at a time, and add them to the pan. Reduce the heat, cover and cook for 2 minutes until the white is just set. Drain.

Serve 2 patties each, topped with the eggs, sprinkled with chives and drizzled with the dressing.

Favourite *Cheesy* STUFFED Mushrooms

 4 *ProPoints* values per serving
ProPoints values per recipe 18

Serves 4
Takes 20 minutes

calorie controlled cooking spray
2 celery sticks, chopped finely
1 large carrot, chopped finely
2 onions, chopped finely
2 garlic cloves, crushed
4 large portobello mushrooms,
    stalks removed and chopped
160 g (5¾ oz) Gruyère cheese,
    grated
salt and freshly ground black
    pepper

Portobello mushrooms are big and juicy; fill them with a mix of celery, carrots and onion, top with cheese and you have a delicious lunch. You can buy bags of ready-chopped veg mix from the supermarket to save time.

Mist a pan with the cooking spray, add the celery, carrot, onions, garlic and chopped mushroom stalks and cook, stirring, over a medium heat for around 10 minutes until softened – add a little water if the mixture begins to stick. Season.

Preheat the grill to medium and place the mushrooms on a non-stick baking tray. Mist the mushrooms with the cooking spray and grill them, stalk side up, for 5 minutes. Top with the vegetable mix and cheese and grill for a further 2–3 minutes until bubbling and hot.

Cook's tip Serve with a zero *ProPoints* value green salad if you like.

CHICKEN & Barley Stew

 4 *ProPoints* values per serving
ProPoints values per recipe 7

Serves 2
Takes 35 minutes

400 ml (14 fl oz) vegetable stock
1 bay leaf
20 g (¾ oz) pearl barley, washed
1 celery stick, chopped
1 carrot, chopped
1 leek, chopped
120 g (4½ oz) cooked skinless,
   boneless chicken breast
salt and freshly ground black
   pepper
finely chopped fresh chives, to
   garnish

This is a simple light stew. You can vary the flavour by adding fresh herbs such as parsley or tarragon or stirring through a little lemon zest and juice just before serving.

Place the stock and bay leaf in a lidded pan and bring to the boil. Add the pearl barley, bring back to the boil, cover and simmer for 15 minutes. Add the vegetables, return to the boil, cover and simmer for a further 15 minutes or until the pearl barley is just tender.

Shred the chicken breast and add to the pan to warm through for a couple of minutes. Season and serve in large bowls, garnished with chopped chives.

 Variation

If you're on a Filling & Healthy day you could make the stew with 20 g (¾ oz) dried brown rice instead of the pearl barley.

Cook's tip Add 200 g (7 oz) new potatoes, halved and added to the stock along with the barley, for an extra 2 *ProPoints* values.

Fabulous Oregano Pork & Ratatouille BAKE

 ProPoints values per serving
ProPoints values per recipe 15

 Serves 4
Preparation time: 10–15 minutes
Cooking time: 1 hour

2 teaspoons olive oil
1 large onion, chopped
1 small aubergine, chopped
1 red pepper, de-seeded and
    chopped
1 yellow pepper, de-seeded and
    chopped
1 large courgette, sliced
2 garlic cloves, crushed
400 g can chopped tomatoes
1 tablespoon tomato purée
1 bay leaf
4 x 100 g (3½ oz) lean pork shoulder
    steaks
1 teaspoon dried oregano
salt and freshly ground black
    pepper

Although this takes a little time to cook, most of it is done in the oven, which means it's really easy to pop on to cook once you're in the door in the evening.

Preheat the oven to Gas Mark 4/180°C/fan oven 160°C. Heat the oil in a large frying pan. Add the onion, aubergine, peppers and courgette. Stir-fry for 5–10 minutes until the vegetables are beginning to brown and soften. Stir in the garlic, tomatoes with half a can of water, tomato purée and bay leaf and season with salt and pepper. Bring to a simmer then transfer the mixture to an ovenproof dish. Cover and bake for 30 minutes.

Remove the dish from the oven and place the pork steaks on top of the ratatouille. Sprinkle them with the oregano and season, then push the steaks down slightly into the ratatouille. Bake, uncovered, for another 30 minutes until the steaks are cooked through.

Cook's tips Serve with 400 g (14 oz) new potatoes, boiled and crushed roughly, with 10 g (¼ oz) low fat spread and some salt and pepper stirred through for an extra 2 *ProPoints* values per person.

To freeze, cool the cooked dish completely, cover with foil, place in a freezer bag and put in the freezer. Defrost overnight and reheat, covered, in a warm oven for 15 minutes.

CHUNKY *Sausage* &
Bean Casserole

 ProPoints values per serving
ProPoints values per recipe 17

Hearty and full of flavour, this sausage casserole is easy to make and the whole family will love it.

Serves 4
Preparation time: 10 minutes
Cooking time: 25 minutes

calorie controlled cooking spray
6 low fat sausages
2 leeks, sliced
400 g can chopped tomatoes
1 teaspoon mixed herbs
1 tablespoon tomato purée
½ chicken or vegetable stock cube,
    crumbled
400 g can butter beans, drained
salt and freshly ground black
    pepper

Heat a large lidded pan, mist with the cooking spray and add the sausages. Cook the sausages until browned. Remove from the pan and, when cool enough to handle, cut each into 3 pieces. Don't worry if they are not cooked all the way through at this point.

Spray the pan again with the cooking spray, add the leeks and cook for 2 minutes until beginning to soften. Add the tomatoes, herbs, tomato purée and stock cube. Half-fill the empty tomato can with water and add to the pan. Season.

Bring to the boil and add the sausage pieces. Reduce the heat, cover the pan and cook for 20 minutes.

Stir in the butter beans, cook for a further 5 minutes and serve in warm bowls.

Cook's tips Serve with steamed broccoli.

Add a 50 g (1¾ oz) chunk of French stick for an extra 4 *ProPoints* values.

Summer *Fruits* ETON MESS

 4 *ProPoints* values per serving
ProPoints values per recipe 4

V Serves 1
Takes 5 minutes

1 meringue nest, broken into small
 pieces
100 g (3½ oz) 0% fat natural Greek
 yogurt
80 g (3 oz) summer fruits canned
 in light syrup, drained and syrup
 discarded

A quick and easy storecupboard pud, great for satisfying a sweet tooth.

Combine the ingredients, place in a serving bowl and eat within 30 minutes.

Cook's tip If you prefer, use fresh ripe strawberries, hulled and chopped, instead of canned fruit and the *ProPoints* values will reduce to 3.

Five ProPoints values

Spring VEG *Spaghetti*

5 *ProPoints* values per serving
ProPoints values per recipe 10

Serves 2
Takes 15 minutes

110 g (4 oz) dried wholewheat
    spaghetti
calorie controlled cooking spray
200 g (7 oz) asparagus, cut into
    5 cm (2 inch) pieces, tips reserved
finely grated zest and juice of
    ½ lemon
1 large courgette, cut into ribbons
1 large carrot, cut into ribbons
2 tablespoons capers
salt and freshly ground black
    pepper

By using zero *ProPoints* value vegetables to make a simple sauce you can have a filling and tasty pasta dish for just 5 *ProPoints* values.

Bring a large pan of water to the boil, add the spaghetti and cook according to the packet instructions.

Meanwhile, heat a frying pan and mist with the cooking spray. Add the pieces of asparagus (but not the tips) and stir-fry over a low heat for 5 minutes until softened. Add a little water if they begin to stick. Transfer to a mini blender or use a hand-held blender to blend the asparagus to a sauce with the lemon zest and juice. Season to taste.

Add the asparagus tips, courgette and carrot ribbons to the pan of pasta for the last 2 minutes of cooking time. Drain well, reserving 3 tablespoons of the cooking water. Combine the blended asparagus sauce and cooking liquid, then return to the pan with the capers and warm through over a low heat.

Cook's tip Add 2 x 125 g (4½ oz) smoked haddock fillets, poached in water for 5 minutes until cooked through, for an extra 2 *ProPoints* values per person.

BAKED Aubergine & Halloumi Parcels

 ProPoints values per serving
ProPoints values per recipe 22

 Serves 4

Preparation time: 15 minutes +
  making the tomato sauce
Cooking time: 15 minutes

2 large aubergines
2 teaspoons olive oil
250 g (9 oz) light halloumi, cut into
  20 slices
fresh oregano leaves
2 x recipe quantities of Simple
  Tomato Sauce (see page 26)
salt and freshly ground black
  pepper

Use your own home-made tomato sauce for these tasty aubergine parcels, cooked in the oven.

Preheat the oven to Gas Mark 6/200°C/fan oven 180°C. Preheat the grill to high. Trim off the ends and slice both aubergines lengthways into long thin strips, aiming for 20 in total. Brush one side of each slice with the olive oil and grill for 1–2 minutes, turning once, until soft and beginning to brown. Season the slices.

Place a slice of halloumi at one end of each aubergine slice. Top the cheese with a few oregano leaves, reserving some for the garnish, then fold over the aubergine strips to cover the cheese.

Place the aubergine parcels in a large ovenproof dish (or 4 individual ones) and add the tomato sauce. Bake for 15 minutes until bubbling. Garnish with the reserved oregano leaves.

Cook's tip Serve with 60 g (2 oz) wholewheat pasta each, cooked according to the packet instructions, for an extra 6 *ProPoints* values per portion.

Loaded *Veggie* NACHOS

 ProPoints values per serving
ProPoints values per recipe 22

 Serves 4
Preparation time: 10 minutes
Cooking time: 30 minutes

2 onions, cut into wedges
6 tomatoes, quartered
1 red and 1 green pepper, cut into
    strips
½ teaspoon olive oil
3 x 42 g Weight Watchers tortilla
    wraps, cut into triangles
calorie controlled cooking spray
½ teaspoon smoked paprika, plus
    extra to serve
420 g can kidney beans in chilli
    sauce
salt and freshly ground black
    pepper

To serve
finely chopped red chilli
4 tablespoons 0% fat natural Greek
    yogurt
fresh coriander leaves, chopped
    roughly

This makes a substantial platter to share with friends when they drop in.

Preheat the oven to Gas Mark 6/200°C/fan oven 180°C. Place the onions, tomatoes and peppers in a roasting tray, drizzle with the oil, season lightly and toss to coat. Cook for 30 minutes, turning occasionally.

Place the tortilla triangles on a baking sheet, mist with the cooking spray and sprinkle with smoked paprika. Bake for about 8 minutes until golden.

Warm the beans in a small pan on the hob and then mix into the roasted veg.

To serve, arrange the tortilla chips on a serving platter, top with the roasted vegetable and bean mix and sprinkle with extra smoked paprika, chopped red chilli, yogurt and coriander.

Chilli *Prawn* STIR-FRY

 ProPoints values per serving 5
ProPoints values per recipe 9

Serves 2
Takes 15 minutes

40 g (1½ oz) dried rice
1 teaspoon sunflower oil
250 g (9 oz) shelled raw tiger
 prawns
1 carrot, cut into thin sticks
1 orange or red pepper, cut into
 thin strips
2 heads pak choi, leaves separated
 and chopped if large
a bunch of spring onions, chopped
120 g (4½ oz) baby corn, halved if
 large
1 green chilli, chopped
1 teaspoon peeled and grated fresh
 root ginger
2 tablespoons light soy sauce, plus
 extra to serve (optional)

Green chilli has a much milder heat than red; if you enjoy more heat, make this dish with a red chilli instead.

Bring a pan of water to the boil, add the rice and cook for 10–12 minutes. Drain.

Heat the oil in a wok or large frying pan. When hot, toss in the prawns and stir-fry for 2–3 minutes until they have completely changed colour from bluey-grey to pink. Remove from the pan using a slotted spoon and set aside.

Return the wok to the hob and add the vegetables, chilli and ginger. Stir-fry for 2–3 minutes until everything has softened and is beginning to colour. Return the prawns to the pan with the soy sauce and rice and give it all a quick stir-fry. Serve in bowls with extra soy if you like.

 Variation

Use 40 g (1½ oz) dried brown rice if you want to make this recipe suitable for a Filling & Healthy day.

Mediterranean HADDOCK

 ProPoints values per serving
ProPoints values per recipe 20

 Serves 4
Preparation time: 10 minutes
Cooking time: 20–30 minutes

60 g (2 oz) pitted black olives in brine, drained and halved
1 tablespoon capers
1 recipe quantity of Simple Tomato Sauce (see page 26)
4 x 150 g (5½ oz) skinless haddock fillets
70 g (2½ oz) fresh white breadcrumbs
20 g (¾ oz) Parmesan cheese, grated finely
1 tablespoon chopped fresh parsley
finely grated zest and juice of 1 lemon
salt and freshly ground black pepper

This haddock dish feels really indulgent with the crispy cheese topping — but it's only 5 **ProPoints** values.

Preheat the oven to Gas Mark 6/200°C/fan oven 180°C. Add the olives and capers to the tomato sauce. Spoon the sauce into an ovenproof dish and nestle the fish fillets in the sauce. Season.

Combine the breadcrumbs, cheese, parsley, lemon zest and juice and scatter over the fish. Bake for 20–30 minutes until the fish just flakes.

Cook's tips To freeze, leave the cooked dish to cool completely, then cover and place in a freezer bag. Defrost thoroughly and reheat in a hot oven, covered, for 10 minutes, then uncover and heat for a further 5 minutes.

Serve each portion with 100 g (3½ oz) boiled new potatoes if you're feeling hungry, for an extra 2 **ProPoints** values per portion.

Smoky CHICKEN in a Pot

5	ProPoints values per serving

ProPoints values per recipe 20

Serves 4
Preparation time: 10 minutes
Cooking time: 45 minutes

450 ml (16 fl oz) chicken stock
250 g (9 oz) butternut squash,
    peeled and chopped
2 carrots, chopped
2 beetroot, cut in wedges
1 onion, chopped
1 garlic clove, chopped
1 bay leaf
4 x 165 g (5¾ oz) skinless, boneless
    chicken breasts
salt
2 teaspoons smoked paprika
2 teaspoons olive oil

Smoked paprika adds a great depth of flavour to the chicken in this recipe. Look out for paprika with different 'strengths' of heat when browsing the supermarket shelves.

Preheat the oven to Gas Mark 6/200°C/fan oven 180°C. Place the stock in a large pan, add the butternut squash, carrots, beetroot, onion, garlic and bay leaf. Bring to the boil then transfer the mixture to an ovenproof lidded casserole dish. Cover and cook in the oven for 15 minutes.

Season the chicken breasts with a little salt and the paprika. Heat the oil in a frying pan and, when hot, add the chicken breasts and brown all over.

Remove the casserole from the oven and nestle the chicken breasts into the vegetables. Cover and return to the oven for a further 20 minutes until the juices run clear when the chicken breasts are pierced with a skewer.

Cook's tips Serve each portion with a 60 g (2 oz) scoop of mashed potato (boiled potatoes, mashed with a little cooking water and seasoned with salt and pepper, if liked) for an extra 1 *ProPoints* value each.

To freeze, allow to cool completely and freeze in the cooking dish or transfer to a freezerproof container. Defrost thoroughly and reheat on the hob in an appropriate container or in a medium oven until piping hot.

The *Best* TURKEY BURGERS

 5 *ProPoints* values per serving
ProPoints values per recipe 20

* Serves 4
Takes 15–20 minutes

500 g (1 lb 2 oz) lean turkey thigh
    mince
1 tablespoon each chopped fresh
    parsley and chives
1 red onion, grated
finely grated zest of 1 lemon
calorie controlled cooking spray
salt and freshly ground black
    pepper

To serve
Little Gem lettuce leaves
cherry tomatoes, quartered
finely chopped spring onion
8 teaspoons sweet chilli sauce

The simplicity of this recipe lets the flavour of the turkey come through – there's just a hint of lemon and fresh herbs.

Combine the mince, herbs, onion and lemon zest in a large bowl with some seasoning. Shape into 8 patties.

Heat a frying pan and mist the patties with the cooking spray. Cook the patties, turning regularly, for around 5 minutes until browned and cooked through. Serve on top of the lettuce leaves with the tomatoes and spring onion, drizzled with the sweet chilli sauce.

Variation
Add a chopped, de-seeded red chilli to the turkey mixture for a little spicy heat.

Cook's tips Serve each burger in a 60 g (2 oz) burger bun for an extra 4 *ProPoints* values per burger.

Freeze the raw patties on greaseproof paper in bags; defrost and cook as above.

RED Lentil Dhal

 Serves 4
Preparation time: 10 minutes
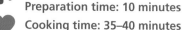 Cooking time: 35–40 minutes

 1 litre (1¾ pints) vegetable stock
200 g (7 oz) red lentils, rinsed
1 onion, chopped roughly
2 tomatoes, chopped
1 green chilli, de-seeded and
    chopped roughly
4 cm (1½ inches) fresh root ginger,
    peeled and chopped roughly
2 garlic cloves, peeled
calorie controlled cooking spray
1 teaspoon turmeric
1 tablespoon garam masala
salt
a squeeze of lemon juice
fresh coriander leaves, to garnish

For the topping
2 teaspoons olive oil
1 large onion, thinly sliced

This dhal recipe has loads of really tasty ingredients – but don't be put off by the length; it really is very easy to make and tastes delicious.

Bring the stock to the boil in a large lidded pan. Add the lentils, bring back to the boil, cover and reduce to a simmer for 30 minutes until the lentils are mushy. Check the water level every now and then and top up if needed with 2–3 tablespoons of water.

Place the onion, tomatoes, chilli, ginger and garlic in a small processor and blend to a paste. Heat a non-stick frying pan and mist with the cooking spray. Add the spices and cook for about 30 seconds. Add the onion paste and cook, stirring, over a medium heat for 2–3 minutes. Stir the mixture into the lentils. Taste and season with salt and a squeeze of lemon juice.

Make the topping. Wipe out the frying pan, add the oil and heat until hot. Add the onion and cook over a high heat for 5 minutes until crispy. Serve on top of the dhal, garnished with the coriander.

Cook's tip Serve with the Winter Vegetable Curry on page 32 for a curry night at home.

Sliced MARINATED *Steak* & Salad

 Serves 2
Preparation time: 10 minutes +
   marinating
Cooking time: 5–10 minutes

250 g (9 oz) lean sirloin steak
100 g (3½ oz) carrots, cut into thin
   strips or grated
2 radishes, sliced thinly
1 small red or yellow pepper, cut
   into thin strips
½ teaspoon black onion seeds
calorie controlled cooking spray
2 handfuls of watercress

For the marinade
2 tablespoons teriyaki or soy sauce
4 cm (1½ inches) fresh root ginger,
   peeled and grated
½ teaspoon artificial sweetener

If you have time, marinate your steak in the morning or the night before and leave it covered in the fridge. Remove from the fridge 30 minutes before you start cooking, to let the steak come up to room temperature.

Combine the ingredients for the marinade in a shallow non-metallic bowl. Add the steak and set aside at room temperature for at least 15 minutes, turning once – you can leave the steak to marinate for longer but cover and refrigerate it.

Combine the carrots, radishes, pepper and onion seeds in a bowl and set aside.

Heat a heavy-based pan and mist with the cooking spray. Remove the steak from the marinade and add to the pan. Cook for 3–4 minutes for rare, 4–5 for medium and 6–7 for well done, turning regularly. Once cooked, remove the steak from the pan and keep warm for 5 minutes. Add the marinade to the pan and warm it through.

Arrange the watercress and carrot mixture on 2 plates. Slice the steak thinly and place on top with a drizzle of the warm marinade.

INDEX

V denotes a vegetarian recipe

PENNY STEPHENS is a cookery writer and food stylist who contributes regularly to books and magazines and enjoys producing tasty and straightforward recipes. Penny has worked with Weight Watchers for over 15 years and has written several Weight Watchers titles. She lives in Hertfordshire with her husband, two children and her dog.